Dance Ministry Basics

Dance Ministry Basics

A Guide for God's Dancers

Lisa Owens

Rivers Publishing
Largo, MD 20775

Published by

Rivers Publishing
P.O. Box 4424
Largo, MD 20775-4424

ISBN 978-0-615-37993-7

Printed in the United States of America.

10 9 8 7 6 5 4 3 2 1

Table of Contents

Dedication

I dedicate this book to the God who is able to do more than I could ever imagine. To God, who looks way beyond my many shortcomings and sees the value deep inside of me. Thank you for not giving up on me. I love you Jesus!

To one of my favorite people, my late and great earthly father, Mr. Aubrey C. Lewis. Thank you for supporting me in all my endeavors and always being there when I needed you. You allowed me to be myself. I am honored to be your daughter.

To my mother, Mrs. Annie Lewis, for your continued love and support, and for allowing me to go to New York City and take dance classes and be involved in all that artsy stuff throughout my life. Thank you today for being a friend and for being an example of a true lady.

To my precious daughters, Ashley and Amber, I really love you. I am so glad God blessed me to have you. You inspire me to stay focused on the prize.

To Prophet and Pastor Betty Bigesby for walking with me through many of my wilderness experiences and teaching me the ways of God. You helped me to understand God better. Your ministry is one of the reasons why I was able to finish this book. Thank you!

My Testimony

In eighth grade I started going to dance classes and training in gymnastics; and I entered my first pageant. Dance seemed to be a natural flow for me. I was pretty athletic and gymnastics was exciting to me.

I was a contestant in my school's pageant and I also was a cast member in my first play, "West Side Story." I loved the stage, the lights, music, costumes, makeup, and the energy that came over me when I performed. I choreographed a modern dance for the pageant and was crowned the Queen. The play was a great success and I knew I wanted to be a star. Broadway, here I come! I was very comfortable on stage. It fit me. It was made for me and I was made for it. Eighth grade helped shape what I was involved with in the years to come.

I enrolled in the performing arts department at my local high school and performed in musicals, dance companies, and more pageants. I loved every minute of it! I received a dance scholarship from the Alvin Ailey Dance Center in New York City, which helped me to rise to another level in my dance training. I attended New York University as a dance major; my first choice was Juilliard, but I did not get accepted. After one year at New York University, I transferred to Howard University where I received a Bachelor of Arts degree. I sat out one semester before entering Howard University. During that time, my cousin invited me to a Bible study that met every Sunday evening. I got hooked because I saw young people on fire for God, full of excitement and energy. I faithfully attended this Bible study. I rededicated my life to Christ and allowed Him to start the process of becoming not just my Savior, but my Lord. My life began to change; and God was beginning to mold and shape me. There was a noticeable change.

While attending Howard University, I decided to run for Homecoming Queen. The contestants had to display a talent, along with other requirements, and I decided to dance. I was sitting in my dorm room and was very frustrated because I could not decide on a song to dance to for the pageant. In my desperation and frustration, I prayed and earnestly asked God to show me what song to choose. Minutes later, I heard a song on the radio entitled "Change." As I listened to the song, I was touched because it exemplified what God was doing in my life. It was as if God Himself said, "Here is your answer;" and that is exactly what He did. It was clear to me. It was a defining moment in my life and I will never forget it. God spoke to me through a song. I said, "That's it. That's the song. I am dancing to this!" Later that day, I asked some friends their opinions and they suggested I dance to something else. All of a sudden, I got confused and the frustration came back. I decided to go back to what God had led me to dance to and the matter was settled. You might be asking, "What is the big deal? She decided on a song to dance to that God led her to. Why spend all this ink on telling us that?" I am spending time on this, because what came out of all of this was something divine.

The night of the pageant came and the auditorium was filled with students. The pageant opened the Homecoming festivities. I stepped out on stage and let go and God, for the first time, danced through me. I had never experienced surrendering my talent to God before. I was always grateful to God for my talent, but I never surrendered it to Him. People in the audience stood on their feet and clapped for a long time. I was told that students were making comments like, "I need to get my life together with God." Others even cried. This had never happened to me before. With all the performances I had done, never were people moved like this one. I realized that God used me as a vessel to get a message across. "Wow," I thought. "God danced through me and I loved being the one chosen for this task."

From that day I decided that I wanted to establish a Christ-centered dance school. I joined a local church's dance ministry and was an active member, but I got to a point where if I did not open this school, I was going to burst. I had to give birth to this baby. Six years later, in 1990, it came to pass. This came after a lot of dreaming, collecting dance materials, praying, and visualizing the school. I named it *Dancers for Christ* (DFC). The dance school trained hundreds of dancers on how to worship God skillfully through dance. DFC blessed many lives over a 10-year period. I received letters from people describing how some of the dances touched them so much that it encouraged them to go on in God. It was a joy for me to be a part of *Dancers for Christ*. Everything has a starting point and that was mine.

In 2000, Dancers for Christ closed its doors and the ministry was renamed *Dance Ministries Unite*. The goal of Dance Ministries Unite is to build, educate, and unite new and established dance ministries through workshops, seminars, and technique and choreography classes.

The Dancer's Prayer

Lord,

Make my life a dance! Choreograph my steps so I know where to walk, where to run, and where not to go. I know that You are the only one who knows all, sees all and can do all, when You want to and how You want to, because You are God.

I need You by my side to lead and guide my feet. Lord, touch my hands so I can clap in celebration of Your goodness. Lord, lift my arms so I can give praise and worship to You.

Lift my head so I can look to the heavens from whence cometh my help. Touch my heart so I am sincere and feel compassion for others. Send me where I need to go, so I can be a blessing to someone else.

Just fill me with Your Holy Spirit, like a breath of fresh air, so I can move when You blow.

In Jesus Name,
Amen

Introduction

Dance, dance, dance! Dance is everywhere! You see dance on commercials. You see toddlers dance when they hear music that moves them. You see dance on videos—people moving and grooving to rhythms. There are a lot more opportunities for dancers today with videos and the various dance shows on television. I have seen how dance has come to the forefront in the secular world. However, many of the videos exploit women. I understand it is money and work for many but, I do not want women to sell themselves as sex objects when they are so much more than that.

Dance is movement. Dance is steps and phrases, dance is expression, and it is an art form. Dance is fun. Dance is a release. Dance is a way to worship and praise God. Dance can be complicated steps or simple movements. Dance is everywhere. It is so natural to tap your foot when there is a pulsating beat playing. You just have a need to join in. I like to bob my head when I hear a beat I like. Others like to snap their fingers. Have you ever watched someone driving in their car and jamming to a song they like? If they could get out of the car, they probably would show you their dance moves, whether you liked them or not. Dance is an expression. It is fun to let go and dance until you cannot dance anymore! Dance can be a beautiful site to see. Have you gone to a ballet and watched the beautiful ballerinas leap with such grace and poise, with so much control and strength? What about watching a man dance with all his might after God has done something awesome in his life and he shouts and dances like David danced? What a site to see!

Dance is powerful. It has the power to set a soul free. A depressed person can be in the presence of anointed dancers and get set free of the chains that bound him or her. Life has its challenges and we need to be ministered to in a variety of ways. Dance is one of them. There was a time not long ago that dance in the church was a no-no to many. "We don't want that here," many have said to me; and years later invited me to lead a workshop. It is refreshing to know that dance is widely received in today's churches. On the flip side, we want to establish a strong, firm foundation, and order so these ministries will stand the test of time.

Do not limit the power of dance. That is why it is important to use the opportunity we have in the church to use this great vehicle to worship God and please Him. It is time to dance! No more holding back. Use what God has given you; it is there to be used to make a difference in someone's life and not just yours. When you choose to sit on your gift, you end up cheating someone else of the blessing they were supposed to get through you.

Chapter 1

Basic Scriptural Foundation

It is important to have a good biblical understanding of the Word of God about how dance was used in the Bible. The Bible says in Colossians 1:16, *"For by Him were all things created, that are in heaven, and that are in earth, visible and invisible, whether they be thrones, or dominions, or principalities, or powers: all things were created by Him, and for Him."* Without God, nothing was made. That defuses the idea that satan created dance. He is not the creator, but he is the one who perverts the truth and deceives those who will listen to his lies. God created dance for His pleasure. The Scripture also says in Colossians 1:17, *"And He is before all things, and by Him all things consist."* I believe the Bible says dance before Him, because He has already gone before us and made it possible for us to worship Him in the dance!

Dance is a form of communication. It is a way we can express ourselves to God through movement. These movements with sincere expression and a pure heart have the potential to touch the heart of God, the dancer and all those who are watching. What an opportunity to give someone hope! When a dance has been touched by God, the yoke destroying power of God creates an atmosphere for worship, celebration, healing, and repentance. This yoke destroying, burden removing power of God, which we call the anointing, is described in the Scripture in Isaiah 10:27: *And it shall come to pass in that day, that his burden shall be taken away from off thy shoulder, and his yoke from off thy neck, and the yoke shall be destroyed because of the anointing.* A dancer who is flowing with the anointing who dances with total abandonment can start a riot in the Spirit, and he or she can change the direction of a service. The altar call could come after the dance instead of having it at the end of the service. People may weep, shout, or even get mad at the devil and start a holy dance. This is so wonderful!

Just think, you invite a friend who normally does not attend church to see a play that your church is producing and you are dancing in it. The play is demonstrating the love of God through Christ's crucifixion and a dancer comes out and ministers a dance with strong contractions, kicks, turns, leaps, and graceful arm movements that carry and loose God's awesome presence and then there is a holy hush, no one moves; and God's presence is so strong that people begin to bow down to their knees and surrender to the Lordship of Jesus. You might be saying, "It's not all that, it's just a dance." But I beg to differ with you, if God really has anything to do with it. There are times when God is nowhere in sight and the flesh is being glorified and the dance becomes a show. I have no problem going to a Broadway show and seeing people perform. But I have a problem going to the house of God and calling something holy when there is no presence of God.

Psalm 149:3 says, *"Let them praise His name in the dance...;"* and Psalm 150:4 says, *"Praise Him with the timbrel and dance...."* Psalm 149:4 says, *"The Lord taketh pleasure in His people...."* God enjoys Himself when we lift Him up and exalt Him. He shows up and begins to perform the necessary tasks that will benefit His people. Have you ever been in a bad mood or been a little down and you decide to talk to God? You begin to tell Him how wonderful He is and you begin to reflect on how much He has done for you. All of a sudden you are lifted up and the heaviness of the burdens you were carrying disappears. It is because God showed up. When light comes, darkness flees.

King David danced before the Lord with all his might in 2 Samuel 6:14. He was celebrating the Ark of the Lord being delivered safely without any mishaps; because earlier Uzzah had died because he had handled the Ark incorrectly. David was ecstatic when the ark reached its destination without anyone being harmed. He was leaping, dancing, and shouting. In Exodus 15:20, Miriam, the prophetess, the sister of Aaron and Moses, took a timbrel in her hand and all the other women followed her with dances in celebration of the children of Israel crossing the Red Sea without harm and their enemies drowning when they tried it. It was a dance of celebration! Would you not dance if God did the same thing for you? Can you count how many times God has parted the waters for you? It was a dance of great victory. It was a release that allowed them to express their great joy.

In Judges 11:34, Jephthah's daughter danced with timbrels because her father returned from war after defeating his enemies. What father would not want to be greeted by his only child? She was celebrating that her father came home alive. I can picture her running and jumping in her daddy's arms and then when he puts her down, her feet start moving and the timbrels start beating. Everyone needs to celebrate when there is a major victory or even a little victory in his or her life or the life of a loved one. In the return of the prodigal son in Luke 15:25, there was music and dancing in celebration of a son's return home after being out there and losing everything and then realizing that there is no place like home. The father threw a shindig! His wayward son came to his senses and they partied. Dance is a release of the emotions that are in the inside of a person; it is an outward showing of what is on the inside. So dance!

The Bible also says in Romans 12:1-2, "*I beseech you therefore, brethren, by the mercies of God, that ye present your bodies a living sacrifice, holy, acceptable unto God, which is your reasonable service. And be not conformed to this world: but be ye transformed by the renewing of your mind, that ye may prove what is that good, and acceptable, and perfect, will of God."* We do not get brownie points because we have decided to obey God and live a lifestyle that is set apart and given to Him. It states that your body is not your own, but it is bought with a price, the blood of Jesus Christ. When Jesus died on the cross for the sins of the world and you received Him in your heart as Lord and Savior, you gave up your will for His will in your life. God is the owner of the property called "you." Therefore, the dancer's heart needs to be pure and tender. It is important to guard your heart and always do a self evaluation. The atmosphere will be affected by you releasing what is in you out of you as you worship and praise God in dance.

What Is Worship

Worship is defined as the reverent love and allegiance accorded to a deity, idol or sacred object. Unlike praise, worship requires a relationship, God seeks worshippers but He commands all living things to praise Him. Worship is intimate and is a private matter of the heart. The best worship we can give God is a lifestyle of obedience, not because it's what we are supposed to do, but because we love God so much that we want to please Him. We should work on our lives being a beautiful worship song to God. Praise and worship is directional. Praise being horizontal reaches out and proclaims God's goodness to others and is the gateway to worship. Worship is more vertical and it is between God and man.

Worship requires surrender and giving of one's self to connect with the Godhead. It is a sacrifice of our total self. There have been many times when I was in worship and in the presence of God and I lost track of time. Most everyone had seated themselves and was ready to go on in the service and I was still in a zone that I did not want to come out. I looked around and saw I was one of the few still standing. To me there is nothing that can compare to being in the presence of God. So much can be healed in worship. Your mindset changes, your body relaxes, and your heart is at peace. Worship dance movements are normally the slower, more graceful movements, but not limited to that. Bowing, lifting arms, kneeling, lunges, waving arms, and graceful leaps are just some of the movements that are fitting for worship. Personally, one of the first things I want to do in worship is sing songs to God. Some of the songs are spontaneous and other times they are songs I already am familiar with. Worship clears the ear gates and prepares you to hear from God.

What Is Praise

Praise means to commend, acclaim, applaud, compliment, hail and recommend, to glorify and exalt. When you praise something you are saying that you approve of it and are celebrating because of it. Praise is an outward showing that will not go unnoticed. It is an act of your will that will have an effect on your surroundings. When a diehard fan's team scores a touchdown, everyone around him will know it. There is a shout, a scream, a clapping of the hands, a stomping of the feet, and a jumping up and down that may occur. There is a great energy exercised in praising. The Bible says, *"Let everything that hath breath praise the Lord"* (Psalm 150:6). The trees, mountains, waters, sun, moon, and stars can get in on this praise commandment (Luke 19:37-40 and Psalm 148:3-120). God inhabits the praises of His people, which means He lives amongst it. God's presence shows up when there is a celebration because of Him. My pastor said something to me one day that made a lot of sense. She said the enemy expects you to pray when times get rough because he expects you to plead with God, but he does not expect you to praise God. Why would you celebrate God when things are not going very well and your back is against the wall? It confuses your adversary when you still have great things to say about God and there does not seem to be anything to praise Him about.

In 2 Chronicles 20:15-26, King Jehoshaphat had to go up against a large army and his instructions from God were to take up his position and see the deliverance of the Lord, do not be afraid, do not be discouraged, go out and face them and the Lord will be with you. He responded by bowing, worshipping, and praising with a loud voice; he listened to the instructions and had faith in God. Jehoshaphat consulted his people and appointed singers to go in front of the army; and they sang and praised God. The opposing army got confused and started fighting against one another and defeated themselves. Not only did they win the fight but they also left with all the enemy's goods. Gold, silver, and other valuables became their property. In Acts 16:25-29, Paul and Silas were in prison and they were praising God so hard that God sent an earthquake that shook the prison doors open. That is powerful praise! That is why the Scripture says, *"Send Judah first."* **Judah** means praise. Judah was one of the tribes of Israel. They were the worshippers and praisers.

Praise clears the air and makes a way for the presence of God. It changes negative thoughts and brings a sense of hope despite the circumstances. Praise knocks down the wall of negativity. When a very energetic and positive person enters a room, he or she brings light and often times by the time they exit the room, if there were any negative people who were present, they are in a better mood. Praise breaks up darkness. When dancers praise God, they should use movements that are big and bold. Marching, clapping, stomping, jumping, leaping, turning, and other upbeat, sharp movements are often used. Praise movements should take up the space well. Do not be afraid to move out and take the space over with powerful movement.

Why Praise God in the Dance?

It is most important to have some valid reasons of why God is worthy to be praised in the dance. I have listed some reasons below. There are not enough pages to list all the reasons why God should be praised. Please add to the list and praise Him!

1. God commands us to.

2. God is Love.

3. God sacrificed His only son so we can have eternal life.

4. God is merciful.

5. God is compassionate.

6. God is powerful.

7. God is the creator of the heaven and earth.

8. God is your provider.

9. God is a deliverer.

10. God is a healer.

11. God has great vision.

12. God is all knowing.

13. God knows every hair on your head.

14. God's positive thoughts toward you are more than the sand on the beach.

15. God is good.

16. God is your protector.

17. God is your anchor.

18. God is Omnipresent.

19. God defeated satan when Jesus died and rose from the dead.

20. God is your peace.

21. God is for you.

22. God has not forgotten you.

23. God has given you the power to forgive.

24. God has filled you with His Spirit.

25. God has given you the power to defeat every demon trying to stop you.

26. God has a purpose for your life.

27. God has given you gifts and talents.

28. God chose you before the foundation of the world.

29. God is your banner.

30. God is your source.

31. God is faithful.

32. God is true.

33. God is dependable.

34. God has given you the breath of life.

35. God has made you a worship vessel.

36. God has gone before you so you can advance.

37. God made sure no one else has your fingerprints; you are unique.

38. God gives you songs.

39. God provides streams in the desert.

40. God gives you peace in the midst of a storm.

41. God prevented you from losing your mind

42. God stepped in and saved you from failing one of your many life tests.

43. God is the master strategist.

44. God sees the greatness in you.

45. God is light.

46. God has placed in you heavenly treasures.

47. God values you.

48. God makes no mistakes.

49. God is always speaking.

50. God hears your cry.

51. God has given you children.

52. God has blessed you with a family.

53. God is a stress reliever.

54. God completes you.

55. GOD IS ALIVE AND WELL!!

I did not mention things like God has blessed you with a home, material possessions, your job, the skill set to accomplish some of your educational endeavors, etc.

As you can see, GOD IS MORE THAN WORTHY TO BE PRAISED!!! IF you really think of all the things that God has done for you, you cannot help but to praise Him! He is constantly giving, watching, and waiting for us to give Him the praise that is due His great name.

Add your reasons to this list:

1._____

2._____

3._____

4._____

5._____

6._____

7._____

8._____

9._____

10._____

Chapter 2

How to Start a Dance Ministry
in the Local Church

Habakkuk 2:2-3 says, "...write the vision and make
it plain upon tables that he may run that readeth
it. For the vision is yet for an appointed time; but at
the end it shall speak, and not lie; though it tarry,
wait for it; because it will surely come, it will not
tarry." This Scripture really ministers to me often.
It says to me, "Have a clear picture of what you see
in your spirit and mind and then write it down." It
also wants you to know that just because you see it
so clearly that you can taste it does not mean that it
will happen right away. You will have to give birth
to that which God has given you. I remember when
I was in labor with my first child. She weighed nine
pounds and one ounce and had a hard time coming
down and out of the birth canal, because of her size.
I pushed for a couple of hours; and then I looked at
the doctor and said, "This is work." He said, "That's
why we call it labor."

Anything that is quality and meaningful and has the ability to change lives requires work. When you get tired you will be required to push; and just when you think you do not have anything left doctor Jesus says, "One more time" and "There it is, the baby is out!" Labor pains are uncomfortable, painful, and annoying, but necessary. This is just to encourage anyone who has tried to get this thing going and it seems like you are pulling teeth. Everyone does not necessarily see it as clearly as you do, that is because God gave it to you and your job is to help others see what you see. When you go to leadership with this idea of a dance ministry, spell it out clearly for them. If you are inspired and excited, it will help others get excited.

Holy Bodies

Living a holy lifestyle has to be a commitment between you and God. In today's world, we are surrounded by many temptations. Many of us have become desensitized to sin and uncleanness because we have accepted, tolerated, and unfortunately embraced the world's system of living. You know the saying, "If it feels good do it." Well, that is contrary to the Word of God. The Bible says, *"Be ye holy as I am holy"* (1 Peter 1:16). This is a command and a requirement in God's kingdom. There should be a difference in the way we live, because Christ should be leading us. We struggle more than we should with this command, because we do not spend enough quality time in the presence of God; and then we wonder why our thinking is off and why negative words come out of our mouths. The flesh is leading instead of God's precious Spirit that lives inside of us. The flesh and the spirit are always warring against each other. If you really want God to be present in your dance, you should bring Him with you. If you have a habit of godly living, God will be evident when you dance. Many times we are doing proper movements, but God's presence is not near, because our lifestyle is lacking God. We are busy running here and there and doing this and that; and when it is time to minister in the dance, we want God to zap us! I have been there many times.

One of the greatest temptations we have to fight against is sexual improprieties. First Corinthians 6:13 says, "...*Now the body is not for fornication (sexual immorality), but for the Lord; and the Lord for the body.*" First Corinthians 6:18 tells us to flee from sexual immorality. All other sins are outside the body, but the Word says that he who sins sexually sins against his own body. I have often wondered about this Scripture. If it is against the body, then it is in opposition to the body. Could that be why people receive different diseases like AIDS (Acquired Immune Deficiency Syndrome), syphilis, gonorrhea, and other sexually related diseases? If it was good for your body, then why do we get diseases? Sexual immorality causes our body to be susceptible to diseases. I know that it is not easy to remain faithful to God in this area. God gave us sexual desires and sex is beautiful, but He commands that it be done according to His standards—between a man and his wife. It is challenging at times, especially if you are single. You have to be watchful of who you hang with, what you watch, and what you listen to. We are inundated with temptations, but if we are serious and committed, we can live a holy lifestyle. You need to have some close buddies whom you can support and who can support you in this. Accountability is a great help.

Let us not just focus on sexual immorality, but let us look at taking care of our temples. First Corinthians 6:19-20 says, *"What? know ye not that your body is the temple of the Holy Ghost which is in you, which ye have of God, and ye are not your own? For ye are bought with a price: therefore glorify God in your body, and in your spirit, which are God's."* We also honor God with our bodies by eating properly, exercising, and getting the proper rest. We need to be good stewards over everything God has given us and He gave us these bodies and we need to see the importance of being healthy. I do not know about you, but when I am sick, I am no good to anyone. I have no energy and do not feel like being bothered with anyone or anybody. I just want to feel better. It is difficult to be sick and be productive. If you can avoid having to take medications and shots, why not?

Philippians 4:8 says, *"Finally, brethren, whatsoever things are true, whatsoever things are honest, whatsoever things are just, whatsoever things are pure, whatsoever things are lovely, whatsoever things are of good report; if there be any virtue, and if there be any praise, think on these things."* Keeping our minds focused on godly thoughts is helpful for the dance ministry in you. We can be moving our bodies in the sanctuary and executing beautiful movement, but our minds can be far from what we are doing. If God commands us to do something, He has equipped us to accomplish it. We have to believe we have what it takes to live a victorious lifestyle in Christ. I love the Scripture that says, *"He who begun a good work in you will perform it until the day of Jesus Christ"* (Philippians 1:6).

Yes, there is a responsibility. God desires for us to be vessels of honor. We are glory carriers. Jesus fulfilled His assignment on earth and now God is waiting on His people to fulfill their assignment. If one of your assignments is to be a minister of the dance, then be excellent in what you do. Do not settle for learning cute dances to Christian music, but dig deeper. God will show you how much greatness is in you and how He can use your gifts and talents to glorify Him.

Preparing to Minister
in a Local Church

Before you minister in the dance you need to set aside some time to bring everyone together. Inform all dancers that at a designated time you will meet for prayer, and maybe to praise and worship God together through song. It is important to get on one accord. There is a lot going on prior to the ministry of dance. Some may have to dress their children, put on make-up, fix their hair, maybe grab a bite of an apple, and the list goes on. You need time to block out everything and concentrate on who you are worshipping and why you are dancing before Him. Do not forget to stretch your bodies. Some ministries stretch together while others do it individually. Do what works best for you. However, I do like stretching together because it is good preparation for dancing together. Many dance ministries also go over some of the dances during this time. This being said, you should meet about two hours prior to ministering, which needs to be arranged and approved by your leadership. You want to avoid as much confusion as possible. Everyone should know the routine of your preparation.

Make sure you have seating reserved for your ministry; work with the ushers on this. All of your belongings should either be in the sanctuary or at another designated place. If your belongings are going to be in the sanctuary, you need to put everything in its place prior to the service starting. Some churches may have enough room for you to place everything in another location except your Bible and what you need for the service. Whatever situation you find yourself in, you need to ensure that there is order and a system that works.

Be discrete and polished in your presentation. Practice your spacing and placement of who stands where prior to your ministering. Try to get a rehearsal in the sanctuary so everyone is familiar and knows where to go when it is time. Some ministries get to have a run-through the morning of and others actually have their rehearsals in the sanctuary or in the location they minister in.

The dancers should be in place and settled at the start of the service. It is very important for the dancers to carry themselves in a way that when it is time to dance they will be received. All makeup, fixing hair, and adjusting garments should have been taken care of prior to you entering the sanctuary. It just looks better when you come in ready and are in order.

Chewing gum and talking should not be a part of the dancers' activities during the service. Having a mint is acceptable, but you should not be chewing gum. When you are seated as a group, people will focus on your behavior outside of you dancing. Be respectful and be attentive to the service.

After you have ministered, decide whether you go out of the sanctuary and gather yourselves, or just go and be seated. The type of dance you ministered and what happened in the Spirit should dictate to you what to do. If many go out to get water etc, do it as a group and come back together as a group, so you do not have dancers in and out; that can be distracting.

As you can see it is about the whole process, not just about what happens when you are dancing. God is a God of order and excellence. Let the entire process be done is a spirit of excellence. Everyone flows better when there is a system in place, it promotes unity.

Dance Engagements

It is good to dance outside the church walls. There are many places that could benefit from this ministry—a women's prison, a shelter, or a senior citizens' home. I took some dancers to a women's prison and they were so moved with compassion they wanted to go back. When you know you are giving someone hope, it does something to the inside of you, if you have a genuine heart. You can also dance at concerts, festivals, and malls. It is also a good idea to find some other dance ministries to which you feel connected. You can dance at each other's churches, have fellowships amongst yourselves, and plan a recital and invite some churches to minister with you.

Times to Dance in a Service

Praise and Worship

There are a variety of ways to dance in a church service. Dancers can minister in the beginning of service during praise and worship. This is for churches that have a praise and worship team. Dancers can dance spontaneously or they can choreograph the movements to the songs. Dancing during praise and worship can be a serious aerobic workout. Get in shape and take rehearsals seriously or it will show when you look like you are going to pass out; or maybe you will pass out. All dancers do not have to dance in all songs. You may rotate people. The leader needs to be sensitive to the Spirit as to when to use what dancers with what songs. One dancer may start dancing to a song and others can join in as they feel a need. Practice in rehearsal. Develop some type of signals so the dancers know how to flow. Many ministries use the "follow the leader" method. This is when one of the dancers moves forward just a little so the rest of the dancers can see them and copy what the leader is doing. This is effective; however, the one leading has to remember that they are leading people and should not throw in surprises and throw off those following. It is just like when you are following someone in a car; and all of a sudden they make a sharp turn and the person following keeps going.

Sometimes the songs are known and practiced to prior to the service, and other times it is spontaneous movement. Both are effective. I have done it both ways and have also combined choreographed dances and free movement. Do as you are led. You do not have to do it the same way every time you dance. It is important for the dance leader to communicate with the praise and worship leader so they are on the same page. The minister of music should know when the dancers are dancing. There needs to be a designated space for the dancers that do not conflict with the singers. There was a time when we used to rehearse with the praise and worship team the week that we were going to dance.

Spontaneous movements when the musicians play

This pretty much is for churches that have a praise and worship team. Sometimes after the team leaves, the musicians keep playing, as if they cannot stop. There is a sound that they play as they are led by the Spirit that can be so beautiful; and a dancer or dancers can dance freely and move throughout the sanctuary. This is one of my most favorite times to dance. It is so liberating to just move until the sound is finished. The dancer senses when to stop dancing.

<u>Dancing a special selection -</u>
<u>a choreographed piece</u>

The dancers will be called on to minister a choreo-graphed piece. Be wise on the length of the piece, because it is not the only activity in the service. So be mindful of the time. You do not want to have someone cut your music or not be asked to dance again. This piece can be connected to the message directly, if you know beforehand what the message is going to be. I never asked the pastor what they were preaching on a specific date. However, I have noticed we flowed right in line with the service just about every time. If you are praying and really seeking God for direction, you will flow with the service.

The choreographed piece could be executed at a variety of times in the service. It could open a service. It could be before or after the offering. It could be after praise and worship, if you have a praise and worship team. It could be before the message or even after it. It could be before communion. It all depends on what type of piece it is.

Types of Dances

Worship dances are normally the slower pieces, with more graceful pieces that could go before the message or before communion; although it is not limited to these. These kinds of movements use bowing, kneeling, graceful turns and leaps, waving arms, lounges, and flowing movements like a breath of fresh air. Worship pieces should move the heart to appreciate and reverence God for who He is. It is loving God just because He is. And the dancers are respectfully using their bodies and mind to give God the worship due to His name. Praise dances can use clapping, marching, running, leaping, stomping, and sharp staccato movements, to name a few. Praise dances are dances of celebration. Praise dance is thanking God for what He has done. There are warfare dances that show movements of war. The dancers are executing movements that can demonstrate pushing through opposing forces. Kicks with flexed or pointed feet can be used. Pulling movements and throwing movements may also be used. There are other types of dances as well.

Costuming Principles

It is very important for the dancers to wear garments that are suited for a church service. The first requirement is that the body is properly covered. Low cut, tight, skimpy costumes that highlight body parts are not appropriate for dancing in the house of God. You want people to be ministered to and not enticed by your flesh. Remember this is not *"Dancing with the Stars."* I love the show, but this is a different venue with a different goal in mind. Fabric that flows when it moves and that is not too heavy is good. Heavy fabric will make the dancers perspire. Polyester is popular for dance garments. When choosing a costume, try to select a style that will complement all body shapes. Many ministries are limited to only a couple of costumes. If that is the case, you want to choose an outfit that can be used for just about any piece. A beautiful siphon gown type garment is nice, but it will complement a graceful worship piece more than an upbeat praise piece. A loose fitting tunic top and wide leg pants in a nice flowing polyester work well. There are so many choices. Some ministries wear a robe—like priestly garments. Others may wear loose jeans and a loose shirt. The costume should complement the choreography. For example, a dance team may wear ripped sheets on top of pants and a top, if they are doing a piece on people in bondage.

Costuming should be creative. Just keep in mind you are in a church. Even if you are imitating "ladies of the evening" for a dramatic, theatrical piece be tasteful on how you portray that. Discretion is a must. I remember dancers from my dance school—I preference that because I had a school and a church ministry at the same time—went to a church to dance and we had a costume with a low back and I felt so uncomfortable. It seemed to be more acceptable when we were on stage at the local high school for our annual recital, but it did not work for the church setting. From that time on, I had them wear leotards underneath that covered the upper back. Undergarments are important. There should be a smooth fit. No panty lines. Men need to also make sure they are supported. Unitards are great to have underneath your garments. These are leotards and tights together in one piece. It covers everything and holds it all together. There should be nothing shaking but a tambourine. You get my point.

Years ago when I started my dance school, I looked through a variety of catalogs and only found a few costumes that were appropriate for dance ministry. However, over the years catalogs now include a liturgical section and there are a lot more choices than there used to be. This is because there is a demand for it. Dance ministries are popping up everywhere. You can choose to have the costumes made. Just make sure the person or persons making the costumes are reliable and will have them finished by the due date and that they look like something you would want to wear. I had a couple of horror stories. Also there are inexpensive stores that have clothing that can be worn. I have seen many tops in local department stores that were beautiful and appropriate and I have purchased them for our youth.

Decide on how to care for your garments. Do the dancers wash their own outfits or take them to the cleaners? Are they left at the church and someone is assigned to care for them? All costumes should be clean and pressed if needed. As for the feet coverings, dancers can wear ballet slippers, jazz shoes, or lyrical sandals. They can even be barefoot. Boots can be worn in a warfare type dance. It depends on your choreography and your surface. You want to make sure the dancer's feet are protected. You would not go to a block party and dance in the parking lot in bare feet. Use your judgment. You can go online and look for dance costumes. There will be listings. The overall objective is to be tastefully covered with a beautiful costume that is suited for a church setting and complements your choreography.

I have seen really good choreography with the wrong costumes; and it took away from the piece. The outfit completes the presentation. Hair is also important. Traditionally, hair was always pulled back and/or pinned up. That still is popular. However, hair should complement the choreography. If you are doing a piece and it is chaotic and every movement is representing a state of confusion, the hair can be all over the place. Basic worship pieces normally have the bun look or flowing hair. There should not be a distraction to the dancer or the audience.

Some Basic Questions to Help You Get Started

1. How many people would you like to have on the ministry?

2. Is there an age range?

3. Is it for male and female?

4. If there are a variety of age groups, do they rehearse on the same day at different locations and do you have enough leaders to handle all the groups effectively?

5. What day(s) of the week will you rehearse and at what time?

6. Where will you hold rehearsals?

7. How often will you minister in the dance?

8. What are the criteria for being a member?

9. What costumes will you wear?

10. Will you purchase the garments from a catalog or store or will you get them made?

11. Is there a policy for wearing jewelry when you minister?

12. What are you requiring for the hair when it is time to minister?

13. Is there a point person designated to call the dancers when they need to be reached?

14. Who is going to choreograph the dance pieces?

15. Do the costumes stay at church or do the dancers take them home?

16. Does the church pay for the costumes or do the dancers?

17. Can dancers join at any time or is there a designated season?

These are basic questions to assist you in setting up a dance ministry. The clearer the vision, the less confusion you will have in your ministry.

How Will You Choose the Dance Team?

There are many ways to establish a dance team.

Option 1

Audition/Workshop

You can hold an audition in the form of a workshop for six to eight weeks. This gives you time to see how committed and serious the people are. Are they on time and consistent in attendance?

- You can teach a basic dance and see how well they can pick up choreography.

- Teach sound biblical teaching on how dance was used in the Bible. You must stress the importance of living a lifestyle of holiness.

- Allow for spontaneous movement. How well do they move without choreography? This is important. What if the music gets messed up and they play something else, can you flow anyway? It is also necessary if the dancers want to dance spontaneously with the musicians.

- Permit the dancers to choreograph their own short piece for one to three minutes. This will allow you to see their creativity and see if you have choreographers in the group.

Group Piece

At the end of the six to eight-week period, put everything together. Have everyone perform the choreographed piece together. If the group is large, break it up and have separate groups perform so you can see everyone.

Biblical Teaching

You could just review your lesson orally and call on the dancers for the answers and see what they have learned; or you could give them a basic test on what you taught. It could be a combination of multiple choice questions, a brief fill-in-the-blank question, and maybe one essay question.

Spontaneous Movement

Call dancers one by one or in small groups and let them move spontaneously.

Dancer's Piece

Let the dancers choose their own music and choreograph a dance for one to three minutes.

This is option 1. I think this way is very effective. It informs those interested that there is a requirement; and if you want it bad enough, you will audition. On the other hand, this may scare many away, if they have not had dance experience. It is up to you to encourage auditioning and let them know that they will be surprised on what they can learn in that short period of time.

Pros

• Weeds out those who are not serious

• Establishes order and challenges the group to work

Cons

- Some who may have been great on the team may not come out because the audition process will scare them.

Option 2

You can allow the 'whosoever' will option. This is allowing whoever is interested to come and be a part of the ministry. This can work; however, you need to have written policies and procedures. The dancers need to know that everyone is required to come to rehearsals and that there is a standard. Make sure you take attendance so you can make everyone accountable.

Even though you have opened the ministry to whomever, you are not required to use everyone for every dance. It is important to establish this rule in the beginning. You may have fifty people who have shown an interest, but only twenty-five are ready to dance. The others need more training. If that is the case, let those in waiting know that they need more time and that when you see that they are ready, they will have the opportunity to dance. Some will adhere and others will become angry and leave. Oh well, that's life. You have to have some standards. If not, you will have a bunch of people running around the sanctuary and it will be a mess. For big services, like Resurrection Sunday (Easter), you should be able to use everyone in some capacity—dancers us-ing streamers down aisles doing basic choreography and other ideas. There is a way to use everyone, but it is not for every service.

The Dance Ministry Leader

Choosing the right leader for the dance ministry is crucial. This called out individual needs to possess some important qualities so that the ministry can flourish. Placing the wrong person in this position will hinder the flow and growth of this special min-istry. This person should see this responsibility for more than just exercise and a good opportunity to be seen. It should not be a chore for them or just something to do. This kind of outlook will trickle down to the members on the team and it will end up being a mediocre ministry. If you are a leader and this is your attitude, it's either time for you to pass the baton because your season is up or maybe you were never called to be in this position in the first place. This ministry is very popular today and many people are flocking to it because it looks like fun and there is nothing wrong with wanting to belong to something that is fun, but please see the importance of this ministry.

You are a minister of the dance. You preach with-out words, unless the piece you are dancing to uses words. The majority of the time it is your face, your body and your spirit that is dancing and we get the message from looking at you if you really believe in what you are dancing to and if you are sincere about the person you are dancing about. I don't want to be too deep and spiritual but, It is a visual ministry, we discern by what we see. If we see an expressionless person that lacks any dancing skill, there is going to be somewhat of a painful experience for the audience. A person may love to dance before the Lord but that does not mean he or she is necessarily called to be on a dance team or dance ministry. It might just be something you do in your living room with just you and God. You might be asking yourself, "How do I know if I am called to this ministry?"

I have a few questions for you: How does dance make you feel? When you hear praise and worship music do you see yourself dancing? Does your body automatically start moving without you even thinking about it? Does movement look good on you? Are people moved when you dance? Are you moved when you dance? Are you good at it? I am not asking if you are from The American Ballet, but can you use what you have well? Can you catch on to the steps? After you know the choreography, are you free to really dance? It should be a flow for you. You should not have to struggle with movement. I am not saying that from time to time it may take you awhile to learn the choreography, but if all the members have picked up the steps and you never seem to get it and they are always waiting for you to get it, I would just see if this ministry is really what you are suppose to be doing. Everyone should dance and praise God, but everyone is not called to be on a dance team or dance ministry.

The leader needs to have an interest and passion for the dance. It is an important part of their life and they should feel a need to put their hands to this plow and be used as an instrument. This person is a planner. They need to see what should happen next. It helps to have a good idea of time. How many rehearsals do they think it will take to learn some of the pieces? They should sense when there needs to be an extra rehearsal or extended rehearsals, if they feel the piece will not be ready in time.

Listed below are some qualities that will assist this leader in being successful.

- **Being committed to God more than the ministry**
  It is also important for this leader to be care-ful not to fall more in love with the dance ministry than the maker of the dance, God. It is so easy to be so passionate and into this dance ministry that God is secondary, because you are so busy perfecting it that God takes a back seat. Many of us have been there. You just love what you do so much that you spend more time perfecting that than perfecting your relationship with God. If you are there, just recognize it and ask God to help you bal-ance this. In time you will put everything in perspective.

- **Be a worshipper**
  A worshipper is one who bows down and submits to God and what is right. A worshipper has a posture of surrender. It is the "Ok Lord, I know I was wrong, do I really have to go back and apologize?" "Ok I will." The worshipper allows God to deal with them, not saying there are not some real times of resistance, but God seems to always find His way back in your heart and mind.

- **Have a heart full of love**
  Love is important for all God's leaders to have. How are you going to lead people without love? People are imperfect and you are imperfect; and if you do not walk in love, you may end up not loving anybody. Love will cause you not to focus on others' faults so much. Love will bring you through the storms that will come and make you remember what is really important and what is not. Love is the key!

- **Attend church regularly**
  Many people come to church and want to join a ministry, but they are not committed to their local fellowship. It's like going to work when you feel like it and when they are giving out service awards you think you are going to receive one, I don't think so. If you are a ministry leader you should be faithful to your house of worship. It is important not to

be all over the place, this church this week and somewhere else the next week and no one knows when you are going to show up. Now it's time to minister and here you come wanting to lead rehearsals and the people and you lack stability. You need to be anchored in the Lord and in your local house of worship.

- **Have a good reputation**
  This is needed. If people do not respect you and you have a history of mess in your life, it is going to be hard for people to receive from you. They say things under their breath like, "Please, are you serious; if she's leading the ministry I am not going to audition for it. I can't sit under her. I just can't see it." No one is perfect, but a negative reputation will stand in the way of people responding positively to you. So be mindful of how you treat people and your actions. People are always watching you; it's just a fact.

- **Pray**
  The Bible says we should always pray. We need to be communing with God as much as we can. Prayer is where God can speak to us and not us just speaking to Him. We need direction if we are going to lead people; and who better to get it from then God, Himself. Pray that God will use you to be a blessing to the people you are assigned to and that He can

trust you to fulfill your assignment in a way that pleases Him.

- **Study God's Word**
  The Word is a lamp to our feet and it will light the way for us. There are so many golden nug- gets in the Word of God, but, it requires some discipline and many of us struggle to study the Word on a consistent basis. We have to make sure it becomes a priority in our lives. God left His Word for instructions on how not only to live this life but to master it, so we need to make it a part of our daily routine. If this is difficult for you, you may have to make sure you have a translation you can relate to and have other books that interest you. There are some great spiritual books that you can read in addition to the Bible. Some dance ministries have a Bible study time included in their rehearsals; even if it is not every re- hearsal there may be designated times when the group studies together.

- **Live a holy lifestyle**
  How are you living? Our lifestyle is who we really are. We live what we believe or what we don't believe. Who are we with? What are we doing? How do we do it? Are we being a good ambassador for God? An ambassador repre- sents he who sends him or her. You should

be able to look at the ambassador and have a very good idea of who they represent by the way they present themselves. It is living what you say you believe. There will be many times when you may want to bail out and say, "Forget it, I don't want to do this anymore;" and walk away, not because you don't love God, it's just that we can get weary in well doing and we want to leave our position for something lower. It's not worth it in the long run. Find time to enjoy your life and your love ones and know when it is time for a vacation, for a change in scenery, and a time to exhale, relax and rest.

- **Have pure motives**
  This is real important. Why do you want to lead this ministry? Do you just want to exercise? Are you bored and just thought this might be fun to do? Do you want to be seen? It is exercise, you will be seen, and it is fun to dance, but your reason for leading this special visual ministry is because there should be something on the inside of you that has a need to dance. Dance is dear to your heart and it moves you and you have a passion for it. You feel that it is just in you to do. It's part of your make up.

- **Have a teachable spirit**
  Every good leader needs to be able to be
  taught. If you think that you "know it all,"
  you are in for a rude awakening. Always be
  ready to learn something new. Your way may
  not always be the best way to do something.
  Just because you are the leader of the group
  does not mean that you cannot learn from
  one of the members on your team. Open up
  and listen, you will learn that there are some
  great ideas that you never thought about and
  should consider and implement. Also if the
  leadership confronts and makes a suggestion
  listen to it before you make a judgment.

- **Be Dependable**
  Can your members count on you? Will you
  show up to rehearsals? Will you follow through
  with the plans you made for the ministry? Do
  they know you will be there come hell or high
  water? When you can't be there, do they know
  that you will make other arrangements and
  they will be notified?

- **Be Responsible**
  This is an extension of dependable; you might
  say they are first cousins. You make sure that
  everything is taken care of for the operation
  of the ministry. You have the songs you are
  dancing to, your rehearsal space is secured,

and everyone knows when there are any changes. You are taking care of your business and things are running smoothly.

- **Be able to receive correction**
  This is very close to having a teachable spirit. You have the ability to receive correction from the leadership over you. There may be times when they feel you or the ministry might be a little off and not going in the direction they may desire you to go. You need to be able to listen and hear what they are saying and adjust if need be. Leadership may not always be right but there is a posture you should have of respect and order.

- **Communicate effectively with people**
  Is your message clear when you speak? The manner in which you deal with people can make or break your relationships. People have feelings and emotions and you should be mindful of that. Learn your members; what you might be able to say to one person may not work for another. Get to know who is on the team, but be fair across the board. If the members genuinely know you care, they will be more open to listen to your instructions.

- **Have vision**
  The leader should see that this is more than just dance steps and have a vision for what

great things can be done through this ministry. You could dance at a shelter or bring children in the neighborhood in for a free workshop. Get with your members and brainstorm
about the creative things you could do in and
outside the church walls.

- **Use Discretion**
  This is crucial for a visual ministry. The type
  of movements and costumes you use needs to
  have discretion all over it. You want to be free
  to create and move, but remember your venue
  and that you need to be tasteful in your selec-
  tions.

- **Be flexible and ready to accept change**
  What happens if you prepared a great dance
  and they did not have time to fit you in the
  service? What if your rehearsal space has to
  be moved because it is needed for something
  else for that day? What if the songs the praise
  and worship team practiced changed at the
  last minute and they did not tell you and you
  have a choreographed piece to all the songs?
  All of the above are real examples of things
  that you may have to deal with. They are not
  life threatening, but they may cause you to be
  frustrated. Take a deep breath, make a sound
  decision, and go with it. Try to keep a positive
  attitude. Even if you are angry, things happen. At the appropriate time, you may need to

address some of the situations, but you need to be able to adjust quickly, and do what is necessary to get the job done.

- **Possess good movement quality**
  The leader should be able to move well. Co-ordination is important. You may not be the strongest dancer in the group; others may dance better than you but you should be able to move well. Movement should look good on you, if you are a dancer.

- **Be knowledgeable of dance**
  The leader should be familiar with different types and styles of dance. There should be a knowledge of dance vocabulary and a skill on how to teach what you know. The leader should take training and classes so they will continue to learn and grow. You can always expand. Go to dance concerts, recitals, and watch dance videos; it will help your creativity.

- **Possess creativity**
  How can you be in an artistic ministry without creativity? How can you use all parts of the sanctuary for a big celebration dance? How can you add to your already existing costumes? Choose a song that challenges you to really find some new movement and the list goes on. Pull on others to help you.

- **Work well with other leaders**
  In a local church there are a host of people you may have to communicate with—the sound person, the choir director, or the ushers. You will have different needs at different times depending on what type of project and or choreography you are doing. When you are asking for assistance, paint a clear picture of your needs and work with what they can accommodate you with.

- **Be able to ask for help**
  Sometimes you feel stuck. The choreography can start looking the same and you need a fresh touch. It is fine to call on some fellow dance leaders and choreographers to come in and sow into the ministry. We all need help from time to time and it is refreshing to have guests to come in and share another view and twist on what you have been teaching. Just make sure you know who you are bringing in, because that can also work against you, if you have the wrong person come in and they bring some stuff that you are not in agreement with. Never forget the input from your members; many will add new ideas and be a great asset to the ministry.

- **Be patient**
  To produce anything of quality, it requires your time, energy, and patience. Sometimes

certain members need more time in their development. Some pieces will take more time than others and you may have to not minister on your designated Sunday, because you are not ready and you gave it all you had, but you know you need a little more time. Just inform the leadership.

- **Train an assistant to lead**
  There should always be someone being mentored and prepared to lead when you are not able. Give the assistant opportunities to lead even when the leader is there. The group should respect the assistant; and much of this respect will be determined by the way the leader endorses their assistant. This needed person is there to help and make sure everything is running as it should. Give them important tasks so they will be equipped when their time comes.

I am sure there are more qualities to list. As you can see, it is less about dance and more about integrity and godly character.

The leader is not perfect—no one but God is perfect. I did not say that the leader is not going to go through some major trials that may have them thinking, *How can I lead anyone with all the stuff I am dealing with in my life?* This called out individual has to be a soldier who will take a licking and keep on ticking. However, Ecclesiastes 3:1 says, *"To every thing there is a season, and a time to every purpose under the heaven."* Ecclesiastes also states that *there is a time to dance* (verse 4), which also means there is a time not to dance. There are times when a leader or a member of the dance team may need to leave for a period of time, if their household is not in order or if there are other reasons that are necessary for them to tend to. It is important to know when to pull back and concentrate more on the home call. If that is necessary, there should be an assistant director who can take over the ministry. However, this does not mean every time life is difficult, you go sit down. Many times God will require that you minister through your storms of life. If the dance leader feels it is necessary to leave the ministry for a period, he or she should talk to the leader to whom they are assigned and get counsel, before they make that decision.

Last Minute Stuff

There will be times when the pastor or leadership will call for a special service or a guest might be coming who was not scheduled previously; and you may be asked to present a dance without the time you would normally have to prepare. If it has not happened to you yet, it will. What do you do? You may get a little irritated, because they put you in a pinch, but lose the attitude that might try to creep in and move quickly to fulfill the request. Think smart!

Do you have something that is appropriate for the occasion? Call the dancers and see how many are available. If they are on the team, they need to make themselves available, if at all possible. If the group is not available or you do not have a piece that fits the occasion, use a strong dancer who has a solo or use a duet or trio. Do what works with the time you have before you. Sometimes these are the most anointed times, because you are so focused and truly depending on God. I have experienced countless times when I did not have the time I would have liked to have had, which made me very focused and I had to go with what came to me. Many times, those were the most anointed dances, because I had to really depend on the God in me.

Real Stories

Deal with situations as they come; and do not let them breed. If you do, one day there may be an explosion. I have had some interesting experiences during my years of dance ministry. I am sharing some of them to give you an idea of some of the issues with which you may be confronted as a dance ministry leader.

I remember two instances when I literally almost got into two fights with some of the members on the dance team. In the first instance, we were at a rehearsal preparing to minister that Sunday. One of the members came in late and I asked her how the piece looked. She responded in a way that caused the atmosphere in the room to spiral downward. There was a new member on the team who had good technique and was learning how to let God use her. She was a little shy and perhaps felt she was not as "spiritual" or as "deep" as some of the "experienced saints." One of the "seasoned saints" made some comments about her that made her feel like she was not worthy to dance. I got real angry and the next thing I knew the other dance team member and I were in each other's face. I had had it! The assistant director of the ministry stood between us and was able to calm the situation. The real reason I was so angry is because I had some suppressed issues with this dancer's ways and how she was able to negatively change the atmosphere of our rehearsals. Leaders, I would say to you, "Confront the issues as they appear, before they get out of hand."

In the other instance, I found myself in the assistant pastor's office because one of the dancers did not want to pull her hair up in a more conservative style. (That was one of our standards.) Their hair had to be in a French roll or something close to it. This is up to the leaders. It is totally optional. Some dancers are beautiful with long hair flowing. The dancer found Scripture about your hair being your glory and other Scriptures about hair. I was not asking them to cut their hair, but just to pull it away from their faces and pin it up when they danced. The assistant pastor listened to both sides and agreed with me. The conclusion was that the dancer had to conform to the dress code that was established. I likened it to a choir director telling everyone to wear blue choir robes on the first Sunday of the month and someone refusing to wear a blue robe, because they wanted to wear a red robe. I guarantee you the singer would not be singing that Sunday. Some things are not that deep. It is just following some of the rules and policies established by the leaders and the group. I do want you to know all of my boxing opponents and I ended up fine; and every single sister I corrected came back later and thanked me. I learned to trust God and be firm without boxing gloves.

When I had Dancers for Christ in my earlier years I was a perfectionist. Everything had to be just right or I was not a happy camper. Once we were having a dress rehearsal for an Army-like warfare dance. The dancers had to wear fatigues with matching hats. While they were putting on their gear, I noticed that a girl did not have a hat. I asked her where it was and she responded that she had never purchased one. The performance was about an hour away. All of a sudden, a loud voice came out of me and I let her have it: "How are you representing being in an Army and you are not in uniform? What is wrong with you?" I was angry and loud and let her know that it was irresponsible. Although it was, I scared everybody. The dancers were scared to breathe. Some of my staff were looking at me like "Lady, it's not the end of the earth." But at that moment, it was to me. Before it was time to go on stage, the poor teenager was crying behind the stage. I was praying that she would not get on stage and break down. She pulled herself together and got through most of the dance, when I noticed that she kept holding her pants up. For a split second, her pants fell down and she pulled them up and the group exited the stage. Well, she and I got through the pre-dance hurricane that I started and we hugged later. She knew she needed to be more responsible; and I learned that sometimes I was a little more intense than necessary.

It is important to build relationships with the dancers away from practice and ministering. Some of the greatest stories I have are of the great times we had outside of dancing. When I had my dance school, Dances for Christ, we had a lot of fun—picnics, pajama parties, trips to the theater, dining at a nice restaurant, etc. I remember one time when we rented an ice skating rink from midnight to two in the morning. All of these activities helped to build relationships; and I cannot forget we gave out gifts at Christmas. You need to have moments when you let your hair down and enjoy one another. We always had great participation and the dancers always looked forward to the next event.

Chapter 3

The Message through Movement

Body Language

Body language is famous for telling a story. Without one word spoken, a person has a perception of the unspoken vessel just by their posture, their facial expression, and even the way they are dressed. You are comfortable or uncomfortable approaching someone by the way they make you feel. They have helped you to paint a picture in your mind. Many times a person's perception is totally wrong. The person who you thought was cold and not friendly ended up being the biggest blessing to you; and the one who you perceived to be the one who would be with you through thick and thin betrayed you.

The Power of Music

Music oftentimes makes dancers and creative people see things. A song could spark an idea for a play. Music can move a dancer to get out of bed in the middle of the night and start choreographing movements. Music helps you to visualize what colors the costumes should be and how the lighting should be. Music is powerful. Music can make you happy or sad. A song can bring you back to an incident in your mind and cause you to love or hate that song, depending on what took place at the incident.

The Power of Dance

Just think! You have the opportunity to paint a picture in someone's mind about the mighty God you serve. You have the opportunity to touch someone's heart, without you physically touching him or saying one word. Your body's movement and facial expressions—that come from your heart—can penetrate someone else's heart and cause them to reach out, cry out, and thank God for His goodness, grace, and mercy. I recently attended a play about God's love and they portrayed what Christ did on the cross. It touched my heart and I said, "God if you could bear all of that pain and suffering, surely I can get through this trial I am facing." I was put in a place in Him where I saw things and my situation through the right perspective. I saw it through God's eyes, and not my own.

We have a great responsibility not to mess up the doors that God has opened for the artist in the church. Almost every denomination has allowed dance in their church. Dance ministries are springing up everywhere. That is a good thing. I believe it is the move of God. However, we have to make sure there is order and a standard of holiness that God will smile upon. Let God use you and your body as a vessel of honor for His glory and purposes and I guarantee you that God will open up more doors for you because He can trust you.

The Variety of Dance Forms

The personality of your church will reflect the type of dances the dance troupe will minister. A young non-traditional church may embrace hip-hop and modern dance, while a more conservative church may favor balletic and/or folk type dances. There is no right or wrong technique. It is the intent of the heart and how the dancers allow God's Spirit to touch their movements that will make the difference. Be careful of using movements that could be enticing to the flesh. Your audience should not feel like they are at a club. On the other hand, do not put yourself in bondage either and think you can only use your arms. God gave you a whole body, so use it.

Prophetic Dance

Some churches only dance spontaneously and do not choreograph their dances. That is fine as well. The musicians may play and dancers may come forth and dance as they feel the Spirit is leading them.

Some people call it prophetic dance—when God gives you the movements and they are spontaneous, not planned. This can be very powerful and has the power to change the atmosphere for God to have His way. The minister could be prophesying and a dancer may use movements to interpret what is being said. There are so many ways to use dance.

My opinion is that a dance could be prophetic and be choreographed. I do not know how many times our dancers ministered a dance that was right in line with the message. It may have appeared that we had a conversation with the pastor and chose the song based on what he shared would be his message, but that was not the case. I also believe that was prophetic, even though the movements were choreographed. There might be a song that you heard and immediately you saw a dance; and for some reason you could not get the song out of your mind. You choreograph a dance and a month later you are asked to dance at a conference and the theme is the very piece that you choreographed. It is relative and I do not think we should put more value on prophetic, or should I say spontaneous dance, than choreographed. Do not limit the God in you. Just move as you feel led. This way you will not box yourself in. God is the author of creativity, so we need not do things only one way.

Dancing through Adversity

There are times when it is difficult to dance and dance maybe the last thing on your mind. The challenges and trials of life can sometimes drain your energy and you feel like you do not have anything left to give. This is when you have to dig deep and pull out the Word of God that is planted in your heart and worship God with a sincere heart and cry out to Him. Some of you might be saying how do you do that? Crying out to the Lord is when you lay everything else to the side and you are determined to reach God and you expect Him to reach you. Your prayer might go something like this:

"God, I need You now. I am tired and if You don't show up, I cannot tell You what might happen. I cannot do this anymore. It seems like I am not getting anywhere and I know I have not done everything right. I know there are some things I still have to get in order, but I am asking You for Your mercy and grace. I need You to come through for me. Lord, I am in need. I love You and I know without You I cannot do this. I will make a mess out of this situation. Lord, what is it I need to do? Should I go over here or over there? The deadline is next week. God I need a word from You now. Lord, Your Word says that you are near to the broken hearted and that You are rest

for the weary. Well, I am weary and my heart is troubled. Save me! Deliver me! I need You, Lord. Your Word also says "Whosoever shall call upon the Lord shall be saved." God I know that is not just talking about salvation, but I also believe You can save me from my enemies. Amen!"

I am letting you see a person who is desperate for God. Have you ever heard Smokie Norful sing "*I Need You Now?*" I am sure that brother sang that song to God when he was crying out to Him for something. You have to talk to yourself and encourage yourself often. Put on some of your favorite worship and praise music and let it minister to your mind and heart; and I guarantee God's presence will show up and change the atmosphere of your mind. The heaviness of the situation will become lighter and you will be able to put everything in perspective. The situation may still be there, but you are able to deal with it in a positive, the God led way.

Chapter 4

Ministering versus Performing

Fast, Pray, Worship

I experienced a major change in my dancing after I started praying and meditating on God and asking Him to use me as a vessel for His purposes. I began to depend on the God in me to move me and I experienced a power and freedom that I did not have before. Prior to that, I had technique and stage presence and I depended on me. After I gave God permission to use my gift, I noticed that my dancing began to touch people in ways that it did not before. They shouted, they cried, and they praised and worshipped God. The difference is that my dancing became a ministry to people's souls and spirit. I could see that God could be Lord of the arts, if you let Him.

When you are preparing to minister in dance, stretch your body, warm up, pray, praise, and worship God. Some ministries fast on a designated day. Do as you are led. You are preparing to be a vessel for godly purposes. Do not just go out and start dancing. You want God's presence all over you so He can change the atmosphere. If there is no relationship with God, you are dancing with limited resources. You cannot give what you do not have. Ministering in dance is like a pastor preaching, but with movement. There is an energy that God gives you. In return, there is a connection you have with Him and the results can be awesome. You do not always have the same results. There are times when you dance and people clap and the service goes on as normal; and other times it is like a fire got ignited and the people rejoiced. Your job is to be available to let God dance through you as you surrender your body to Him. Forget about "How do I look doing this movement." Just move. Step out on faith and believe that for those couple of minutes, you carry the message needed and everyone is waiting for you to release it. You are a carrier of His glory and God does not want to share His glory with anyone. Lucifer tried that and God kicked him out of heaven. I have seen great execution and showmanship by a dance ministry, but it was missing the presence of God. I have also seen very simplistic dances by dance ministries and because God's presence was on them, they moved me while the others did not. My opinion is that it is important to have both some skill and the anointing. If God's presence does not show up, it is just a nice dance to Christian music, which is probably the most popular.

When you are trained and have technique, you have to check yourself and make sure your motives are pure. It is easy to slip into "Look at me." If that happens, just ask God to help you die to self

exaltation. God is faithful and will help you accomplish this. On the other hand, I do not think someone who is skilled should not hold back because they
are trained and possess some technique. There are
times when the group you might dance with is not
as technical as you and you feel the tension of their
insecurity. Just hang in there and use what God has
given you and assist in helping the others. If you are
not the leader, avail yourself to the leader to help
teach technique. There may be cases when the leader is not as technical and may not receive the skilled
person, because they are insecure. If that is the case,
pray and wait for God. He has a way of dealing with
His children. But when it is time to break loose, allow what God has blessed you with to be a blessing
to others. If you can kick, kick! Do what you do. Just
do not show off! Minister through the power of God
and see how you will touch others.

When you are truly being used as a dancing vessel, movements will come to you at times that you
did not choreograph. You may end up in a pew standing right in front of someone. There is a power that
will come upon you that demands darkness to flee
and light to come. Your body will use the space to
accommodate all the movements that come; and the
space seems to extend to allow you to use all the
movement. You will be surprised at all the movement you can get in a small space. When you are
flowing, you forget about the space limitations. The
freedom in you makes your body move. Ministering
through dance is allowing the Spirit of God to come

out and change the atmosphere and cause hearts to be touched, because His heart is touched. God is awesome. You think, *Lord how can you use someone like me* and God says, "Because you are fearfully and wonderfully made. Just yield." He then can take you and put you on display for His Glory! God is awesome.

When you really think about it, it is an honor to be chosen to be a vessel for God. After all, He is the Creator of the universe and if He desires to use you, it means He sees something in you. Just remember that if God sees it, that really settles the matter. But you have to receive it. Many times we are overlooked or labeled but God knows what is in us. Stay focused on what God told you about you and you will succeed. We get in trouble when we listen to other voices and it crowds out the truth. The truth is God loves you and sees the value in you. Do you?

Chapter 5

God's Free Dancer

If you are going to be a free dancer, you must forgive and let go of the things that God has impressed upon your heart to release. God sees way beyond the present and knows the damage that continuing in something He has told you to let go will do to you and in turn others who are assigned to you. Disobedience is a huge hindrance in your freedom. The only true way to be God's free dancer is to live a surrendered life—surrendered to God. This is not an overnight process. This comes from trial and error. There will be times you thought you were surrendered, only to find out you were not.

Trials have a great way to locate where you are in your walk with God. If every time the trial you are facing brings you back to the same mess God has delivered you from, you need to do a self evaluation. Ask yourself, "Why is it every time I go through something challenging, I "act up?"" I forget about taking a deep breath and digging within and allowing the God in me and the Bible studies, Sunday services, and conferences that I attended to make a difference in my life. You have to talk to yourself and allow everything to be put in the proper perspective.

You need to say to yourself, "I will not die, but live and proclaim what the Lord has done." Unforgiveness is a hindrance to everyone. It is a heavy burden. It kills your joy. It stifles you. It is bondage. God has forgiven us for our sins and died for us knowing the ugly state we were in. If God can forgive, why cannot we? When Jesus was on the cross, hanging there in excruciating pain and dying, He said to the Father, *"Forgive them for they know not what they do."* (Luke 23:34). People spat on Jesus, called Him the Prince of the devils, whipped Him, and crucified Him. Jesus had compassion on them and forgave them. If that is not the love of God, I do not know what is.

You can really dance freely when you have allowed God to deal with your issues and you acknowledged that you need Him. You can be God's free dancer when you have learned to love who God made you. The Bible says, *"You are fearfully and wonderfully made"* (Psalm 139:14). You are no longer trying to please everyone, but are at a place where you say, "God, it is You and me. As long as You are leading, I will follow."

Dance your way to your freedom and in return you will free someone else. That is why it is never just about you. When you are operating in what God has called you to, the people assigned to you are ministered to because you have what they need. They are waiting for you to come forth. You have no idea how many people are praying that someone like you would come into their life. You have no more time to waste. No more excuses. It is over. Give it up so you can begin to fulfill your great destiny. God has gigantic plans for you. He is just waiting on you to line up. Your freedom is tied up in your obedience to God. If you submit to His will and just trust Him, you will begin to see yourself blossom and doors will open because you are in position. There are no short cuts. It is God's way or you are going to end up short.

God's free dancer is full of energy and excitement with power to kick down ungodly spirits. When you turn, you loose hope; when you jump, you loose victory. Your presence just standing there waiting for your dance to begin is powerful; because God's free dancer brings God's power and releases it to those who are watching. God's free dancers are precious to Him and He greatly values them. If nobody has said it, let me say it, "You are special, beautiful, talented, and powerful. God appreciates you and so do I. So, dance, dance, dance!"

God's free dancer focuses and concentrates on what God said about them. When it is time to dance, put all concerns under your feet and get lost in the presence of God and allow His presence to take you into heavenly realms. There is a focus and concentration that is necessary to get there. Many events often happen before it is time to minister in the dance. The children may act up and your husband or wife may have plucked the only nerve you seemed to have left, and now you are supposed to dance and be a blessing; but all you feel like doing is crawling under a rock. The bills are due and you do not have all the money to do what you need. The pounds you promised yourself you would lose before you danced again are still on you and the list goes on. My suggestion to you is dance anyway. Give it all you have got anyway. Get into God's presence by concentrating on His greatness and bowing your heart and dancing with your body and soul.

Even though you may be in God's presence, you still have to be aware of the other dancers, your space, and the choreography, if it is a choreographed piece. However, there are times when the choreography goes out the window and movements come that you did not plan. Give it your best shot; forget about "How do I look doing this movement." Just move! Step out on faith and believe that for those couple of minutes, you carry what people need. You are the deliverer of the message needed and everyone is waiting for you to have the solution. You may not think a dance can be all of this, but people have come to the altar for salvation after an anointed dance (a burden moving, yoke destroying dance) that is touched by God. You are a minister of the dance. You deliver the message. You just do it without talking unless the choreography has words in it spoken by the dancer.

God's free dancer is not loaded down with sin. I am not saying you are perfect and do not have struggles, but you are walking and living in a lifestyle that is acceptable and pleasing to God. Premarital sex, unholy conversations, backbiting, strife, and foolish behaviors are not a part of your lifestyle. You do not practice these things. Remember, I am talking about "God's free dancer." How can you be free, if sin is loading you down? Sin is a heavy weight and a free dancer is light and travels through space without the load on his or her back. His dancer has decided to take a stand for a pattern of holiness and righteous living. His dancer repents and turns away from sin after he or she has done something displeasing to God. They have a pure heart and when they are not right with God, they are uncomfortable and have to get right with God or they are miserable. God wants to give you an abundant life.

The free dancer is like a breath of fresh air and allows her or his body to be used unselfishly—arms, legs, torso, facial expressions, feet, and, most importantly, with the whole heart. You have allowed yourself to put everything to the side so you can move without the weight; the only weight you want to experience is the weight of His glory!!! Now that is heavy!!

Free to spin, free to jump, free to clap, free to wave, free to leap, free to contract, free to kick, free to bow, free to stretch, free to be you! It is liberating to finally get to the place where you totally accept who God made you to be. God has uniquely designed everyone for a specific purpose. It was He who gave you the gift of dance. So dance, why don't you! Stop worrying about what you do not have and celebrate and use what you do have. There was a time in my life that if something was not perfect in a dance, I would really go through major tripping for the rest of that day. Those days are over. Now, I say, "Oh well, what are you going to do—been there, done that." You will wear yourself out, and at the end of the day, it really did not make much difference. You have to learn to get over it. Every dancer and dance is not always going to meet your expectations. That is life 101. Better learn now and save yourself some major headaches. It is not deep. Do your best and that is it! *He whom the Son sets free is free indeed* (John 8:36).

So let God take what you have, no matter how big or how small, and use it to touch other people's lives. You have so much in you to share and the sooner you believe what God has said about you, the quicker you can be used to be a blessing to others.

Chapter 6

Poems for Dancers

Connection

Lifted hands attached to graceful arms
Pointed feet accompanied by strong legs
Extended arms connected to relaxed
shoulders
Palms turned to the sky with a lifted
head
The dance connected to the heart
Your renewed spirit connected to God
What a beautiful sight to see
What a dance to behold

Spin

Turning around with grounded feet
One foot and then the other
1, 2, 3, 4
This is fun
You better spot or you'll get dizzy
Oh no, there's the wall
Are you all right?

Stretch

Lifting up and over
Extending everything you have
God stretches us just like movement does
Reach hard and return to your position
Exhale and relax
Up and over
Stretch till it hurts
Stretch till it feels good
Stretch so when the choreography of life
comes
Your flexibility will protect you from
injury
Stretch, stretch, stretch

Whip It

Whip your flag
Make the enemy mad
The enemy is bound to the ground
Keep him down
Whip it, whip it, whip it
The sound of war
The sound of victory
The sound of peace
Whip your flag
Make the enemy mad
Change the atmosphere
Clear the air
What a wonderful way to make the
presence of God appear

Just Imagine

Just imagine being free as a bird
No burdens, no weights
Just moving through space
Grace through space
And finishing your race

Run, Jump, Leap

Run, jump, leap
Clap in defeat
You win, you're the victor
Once again
He tried to hold you
He tried to scold you
But you win
Because God is within
In where, you may ask
In you
He's in you and He's everywhere
Run, jump, leap
Clap in defeat
You win, you won
And the fun has just begun
Run, jump, leap
Clap in defeat
You win, you won
And new life has begun

Write Your Own Poem

_____

_____

_____

_____

_____

_____

_____

_____

_____

_____

_____

_____

_____

_____

_____

_____

_____

_____

_____

_____

_____

Contact Information

The author is available for workshops, seminars, retreats, or wherever help is needed in setting up and managing a dance ministry. She can be reached at:

Rivers Publishing/Dance Ministries Unite
P.O. Box 4424
Largo, MD 20775-4424

You may call her at: 240-206-9370

Visit her website at:
www.danceministriesunite.com

Send a message to:
lisaowens4606@comcast.net

Join her on Facebook at:
www.facebook.com/danceministriesunite

And on Twitter at:
http//www.twitter.com/Rivers234

Psalm 139:
You are fearfully + wonderfully made.

CPSIA information can be obtained
at www.ICGtesting.com
Printed in the USA
BVOW09s1602070318
509943BV00028B/1484/P

9 780615 379937